Creating a Concierge Service for Seniors

An Experience Based Guide

Embrace the Opportunity to Help Others <u>and</u> Make Money

Debra Hadsall

"It`s not how old you are, it`s how you are old."
Jules Renard

Creating a Concierge Service for Seniors
An Experience Based Guide

Copyright © 2013 by Debra Hadsall

ISBN: 978-1-304-49088-9

All rights reserved. No part of this book shall be reproduced, stored in a retrieval system, or transmitted by any means, electronic, mechanical, photocopying, recording or otherwise, without written permission from the author.

This guide contains the opinions and ideas of its author. It is intended to provide helpful and informative material on the subject matter covered. The author and publisher specifically disclaim any responsibility for any liability, loss, or risk, personal or otherwise, which is incurred as a consequence, directly or indirectly, of the use and application of any of the contents of this book.

For information contact: financialfreedomparty@gmail.com

INTRODUCTION

My husband and I created a senior services business. The best way we could describe what we provided for senior citizens was to refer to it as a lifestyle concierge service. This guide is designed to share with you our experiences and business approach. We had no roadmap, only our business background along with a new found experience of living around a concentrated number of seniors.

This business was the product of necessity. We had moved from a large metropolitan area with an inter-generational population, to a small and somewhat isolated resort town on the coast of the Gulf of Mexico. The population there has a heavy concentration of retirees and older folks, some who live there year around, and others who visit throughout the winter. Coming from a large city meant we had to adjust to the business needs of a smaller resort town with a different demographic. As with many of the locals, we found it necessary to build a schedule of part-time incomes. Even before the economy tanked in 2008, the area we lived in lacked any full-time jobs with incomes like those in the big city. We learned to really tune into the needs of those around us and to use our skills, abilities, talents, and experience to deliver something they would "buy". It had never occurred to us to work with seniors until we saw how strong the need was in the community.

We had relocated for what we expected to be a temporary stay due to the health of one of my parents. Over time we decided the warm weather in the winter was really nice and our stay was extended. In the process we lived in a resort and began our experience of living in a community of seniors and caring for my family members who were seniors. It became very apparent that the natural aging process, sometimes combined with medical challenges, affected the ability of seniors to maintain their independence. We also belonged to a local church with a median age of 72. Everywhere we went the lives of seniors were on display. Our crash course on helping and understanding them had begun.

Not everyone can work with seniors, just as not everyone can easily care for babies, children, teenagers, or even their own family members. It just isn't for certain people. However, my husband comes from a family who was raised on the farm and elders were given special reverence. It is just in his DNA and a gift. He has a kindness and patience with them that is natural. He saw the value of offering his services to seniors and their families. So, it was easy to transition into this type of work since we had been doing it for my family members.

We chose to keep this business as a part-time source of income. It fit easily into our daily work schedule and by having 2-3 clients we could balance their needs while still fulfilling other business obligations. However, the demand for senior services was growing and with a little more effort the business could have easily expanded. The interest in our services from both seniors and their family members (who usually lived hundreds of miles away) was encouraging. Our business was totally referral based. Had we chosen to advertise and reach out more in the community, the business would have grown.

One of the biggest surprises we continue to experience is the interest other people in different parts of the country have in the concept. People are genuinely concerned about the safety and welfare of senior citizens. The need to aid seniors has a significant impact on families, communities, and service agencies such as social services or even medical care providers. This can be costly both financially and emotionally. We have even heard of someone else starting a business based on our model after learning about it from the son of one of our clients. Others who have cared for family members have encouraged us to share the concept. These are adult children who have struggled with concerns about the safety, security, and happiness of parents as they age.

Please don't underestimate the value of the information shared in these few pages. It is a summary of the work and experiences which occurred over five years. We learned that assisting seniors is a hands on activity with people who are experiencing a lot of different emotions and feelings at a new stage in their lives. This involved us interacting with them on a consistent basis, lots of conversations, a little negotiation, and plenty of active listening. We learned a lot from them and most of the things we tried worked very well. A few things we learned not to do again, but fortunately they did not have costly consequences. However, it certainly would have been nice to have a guide like this to give us ideas and moral support.

We saw the need for a senior services business in the community where we lived. You may be having the same experience where you live. The market for a concierge service for seniors varies by location and you may need to adjust your business model. It would have been more difficult to have this business when we lived in the large city with a smaller proportion of seniors in the overall population. However, as you spend a little time listening to those in the community you wish to serve, you can see if the need is there and make a decision about whether or not it can be a profitable business.

You will need to seek legal guidance before you use agreements or develop policies for your location and clientele. Additionally, you will be running a business and the normal requirements for establishing a business entity, bookkeeping, taxes, etc. apply. These are all activities which can be learned easily elsewhere so they are not covered in depth here.

The terms concierge service and senior services are interchangeable in the context of this guide. Also, the terms concierge and service provider also carry the same meaning. We chose not to use the term caretaker since it describes a different level of care than that of a lifestyle concierge.

Best wishes for success as you consider this as a service to others and a business with potential financial reward.

Debra J. Hadsall

Table of Contents

Introduction		i
Chapter 1	What is a Concierge Service for Seniors?	1
Chapter 2	Why Would Seniors Need a Concierge Service?	3
Chapter 3	Types of Services	5
Chapter 4	Clients	6
Chapter 5	Skills of Service Providers	9
Chapter 6	How to Market	11
	Example of Information for Basic Brochure	14
Chapter 7	Legal Issues	15
Chapter 8	Business Practices	
	Privacy of Client Information	17
	Visit Logs and Accountability	18
	Service Agreement	19
	Example of Letter	21
Chapter 9	Closing the Deal	23
Chapter 10	Making Money: Pricing, Income, and Expenses	26
Chapter 11	Blog Website with Static Pages	29
Chapter 12	A Few More Tips	43

CHAPTER 1
WHAT IS A CONCIERGE SERVICE FOR SENIORS?

Generally, a concierge provides a personalized service for customers. Most of us are familiar with hotel concierges who help the guests by recommending restaurants, giving directions, obtaining tickets to shows and events, and generally making life easier on the guest. This service is provided with the expectation of payment to, and financial reward for, the concierge. The payment part is important to understand because some guests may expect to benefit from the time, expertise, and attention of the concierge without the expense.

A concierge service for seniors targets a specific group of people in a specific locale and is designed to meet their needs. The ideal client is one who is capable of living independently, but wants someone else to assist with activities such as:

> A concierge service for seniors often allows a person to remain at home or in familiar surroundings. As the senior's medical needs change and become more significant, the care shifts from the concierge to medical providers.

- ❖ Locating a housekeeper
- ❖ Shopping for groceries
- ❖ Bill paying and checkbook monitoring
- ❖ Setting up medical appointments and being a medical buddy
- ❖ Coordinating with maintenance providers
- ❖ Mailing and picking up letters
- ❖ Performing routine tasks like changing light bulbs or taking out the trash

Additionally, one of the most important qualities of a concierge service for seniors is the scheduled and consistent contact with the client. This day-to-day physical contact allows the concierge to contribute to the safety and well-being of the client. Any changes in appearance or behavior become readily apparent. Small projects, such as getting on a ladder to locate an item in a cabinet, can be performed safely by the concierge. Knowing someone is coming regularly gives the client comfort and encourages her or him to rely on the concierge for tasks which can result in injury or confuse the client (such as paperwork).

A lifestyle concierge service for seniors does not provide medical care. Often a concierge service for seniors provides an interim solution for those who can live independently with some assistance from the concierge, but then the senior moves on to retirement communities, assisted living, medical care facilities, or being cared for by family. There are signals which will help the concierge service, the client, and the client's family determine that the level of service needed is outside the scope of the concierge. These will be mentioned later in this guide.

There is an exchange of time and talent for money. As stated earlier, a concierge provides a service for financial reward. There is considerable value added to the clients of the concierge service and this value comes with a cost. Often the activities needed by seniors are provided currently at no cost by neighbors, family members, or faith communities. This can lead to the expectation by the senior that he or she is entitled to services and that they should be performed for no cost, or for a nominal fee. A concierge service for seniors provides services to clients who can afford the level of care provided, can see the value of what they are getting, and agree to use their resources to purchase the service. Usually the fees are paid by the client, but family members may wish to cover the cost.

CHAPTER 2
WHY WOULD SENIORS NEED A CONCIERGE SERVICE?

Let's begin by acknowledging that the term "seniors" means different things to different people. There can be a wide range in ages for the category" senior citizen". Some marketing campaigns identify 55 as the beginning of being a senior. Others start at age 62 and others at full social security age around 65. People in the 55-65 age groups tend to think of seniors as being in their 70s, 80s, and 90s and beyond. Experience shows that the need for assistance from others is often affected more by the physical and mental capabilities of the individual than a set age. However, you can expect that most of the clients for a concierge service for seniors will be in the 70+ age group. There are always exceptions of course.

Seniors are no different from the rest of us. They prefer to stay as independent as possible. While some are comfortable moving into professionally managed facilities such as retirement communities or assisted living, many are not. They can become adamant about not moving, even if it endangers their lives. Historically parents moved back in with their grown children for care when they could no longer live alone. Also, it was (and is) quite common for family members to provide daily or periodic care for older family members. Logistically this doesn't always work in our society because parents and children are often separated geographically. Interestingly enough, sometimes parents choose to retire to areas which not only have better climates, but also as a way to separate themselves from unpleasant family situations.

Adult children have their own lives to lead, families to raise, bills to pay, and lifestyles. Often they are not willing to take on the role of caretaker or they are not able to easily pack up and move to be with the parent or parents. Let's face it, caring for seniors isn't for everyone, no matter how needed it might be. This is where a third party concierge can become part of the solution.

REMEMBER

Senior citizens are not defined by some title. Each person is an individual and her or his needs have more to do with physical and mental capabilities than just a date of birth.

Families and friends may not always be the best service providers.

The easiest and fastest way to serve senior concierge clients is to cultivate clients and relationships with seniors who live in resort, retirement, or other socially contrived communities. They market for you and their friends tend to be more concentrated geographically. Less travel time and lower marketing expenses equate to a lower operating cost. This savings benefits both you and your clients.

Be emotionally prepared to turn down potential clients who can't afford you. Offer them a list of solutions including social service agencies, local non-profit assistance; and encourage them to reach out to their faith communities and families.

The need is easy to see in areas with large concentrations of seniors. As mentioned in the introduction, my husband and I started a concierge service for seniors in a resort area which is located near the Gulf of Mexico. This is an attractive retirement and tourist area because of the semi-tropical climate. It also means that virtually all the seniors are from "up North" and isolated from family support. Even so, they have come to expect a certain lifestyle. Some can afford to purchase assistance to maintain that lifestyle. Others leave to return to be with family while some rely on local friends and faith communities to care for them. Of course that reliance doesn't always work out as people tire of caring for seniors on a volunteer basis, the senior can become difficult to deal with, or the concentration of seniors is larger than the number of younger people to help. Our experience is that the need for a concierge service for seniors is easily recognized in resort areas where there are concentrations of older people living together in a community, park, or some other socially contrived living arrangement. For a concierge service to be profitable, these communities should have residents who are financially comfortable and can afford more than just the basics of day-to-day retirement living.

Examples of types of services which appeal to seniors are listed on the next page.

CHAPTER 3
TYPES OF SERVICES

Home helper services and errands
Provide medication reminders
Pick up prescriptions
Assist with laundry
Change linens
Assist with planning and preparing menus
Arrange appointments
Take out garbage
Write letters and correspondence
Ensure appointments are met
Organize and clean closets and cabinets
Accompany to lunch or dinner or events
Escort to religious services
Assist with pet care
Shop for groceries
Care for plants
Conversation and companionship
Respite care for caregivers
Provide reminders for appointments
Mail bills and letters
Plan visits, outings and trips
Make plane reservations
Maintain calendar
Supervise home maintenance and interact with contractors
Monitor diet and exercise
Check food expirations
Assist with evening/morning routines
Maintain records of life events
Establish automatic bill paying or assist with submitting payments
Reconcile bank statements
Monitor insurance bills and payments

> **REMEMBER**
>
> *Clients will not need, or be able to afford, all these services. This list is a way for them to understand how having you as their concierge can improve their lives. You can delete or add activities based on your business capabilities and the local needs of your clients.*
>
> *If a client's needs grow dramatically and more items from the list are added to his or her services, there will be a resulting increase in cost to the client. This could also be a* **signal** *that a concierge service no longer meets the client's needs. A discussion with the client and family member will become necessary.*
>
> *Routine is very important. Seniors do not like changes in their daily schedules and if you are going to change a time or way of doing things, communicate clearly with them in advance. Sometimes clearly means leaving a note, making a follow-up phone call, or giving a reminder right before the appointment or activity.*

CHAPTER 4
CLIENTS

This guide continuously emphasizes the importance of understanding and serving the needs of clients who are senior citizens. Sometimes it is easy to provide them the services as agreed upon, but often aging and the accompanying physical and mental changes of seniors can lead to misunderstandings, hard feelings, and service problems. To improve the chances that your services and your clients are a good match, please consider the following:

Potential Clients

Age alone is not the best criteria in determining if a concierge service is appropriate. When meeting with potential clients it is good to learn about their habits, needs, and existing support systems like family, friends, and others. Part of the process is to be honest with them in terms of the costs and value of your services. Yes, there is some selling in the process of screening clients and coming to an agreement between the two of you (and sometimes a family representative). More information about the agreement can be found in Chapter 8.

The physical and mental health of the senior are the biggest things to consider. Our experience has been that the physical health challenges and limitations are pretty easy to learn from the senior. Most are apparent and if they aren't, we found seniors to be forthcoming during the interview. This is not true when trying to understand how much the senior easily and quickly understands in terms of day-to-day living and more complicated things like driving a vehicle, paying bills, negotiating with maintenance providers, communicating with doctors, writing letters, etc. Cognitive abilities are hard to evaluate. The client is often in denial or unable to grasp that changes are occurring. Families often don't want to accept the fact the senior has a cognitive impairment. You can objectively assess if the client will be a good fit for your business.

Current Clients

Current clients tend to get into a comfortable routine and everyone understands their roles. This creates a good rhythm for the client and the service provider. Maintaining your client base is important and requires doing small special things for your seniors. It is nice to be able to give a client a card on her or his birthday, drop by with a small holiday gift, or take a photograph and email it to family members. There are other low cost or no cost fun things to share with your client who is functioning well with a little help from your service.

All is usually well, until something changes. Changes can come very quickly. It could be a change in physical condition due to illness, a fall or other accident, or just the normal aging process. Difficulty by the senior in understanding and mentally processing things which used to be easily accomplished may be the result of a new health concern. You may be one of the first unbiased and consistent observers of this type of change. It is very tricky to sort out what is causing it. Even professionals may not be able to instantly determine if it is dementia, Alzheimer's, or any other condition. We learned that no matter what it is called, the change makes the life of the client and the service provider more difficult. The service provider will probably end up dedicating more time to fulfill the client's needs and find the new work requirements are adding up and getting outside the scope of the agreement. This is not good for the client and not acceptable to the service provider. It will become necessary to consider conferring with the family representative to work out a resolution. The client may need to move to a higher level of care (such as a retirement community, assisted living, etc.) and you may find a need to terminate the agreement after coordinating with the family representative.

We chose not to accept a client if we knew he or she already had great difficulty with cognitive processing, or if there was evidence of behaviors we had experienced earlier as a service provider to someone who had dementia. If you aren't knowledgeable about these cognitive conditions, you may want to become aware of some of the behavioral characteristics. In your business you will know something is up when tasks on your list grow because the client can't master them anymore and it takes her or him three or four times longer to perform tasks than it used to. These are just some examples. A lifestyle concierge is not a medical care provider. Fortunately the medical industry has a wide variety of caregivers who are trained and qualified to care for seniors needing medical care. We found that sorting out the client's level of mental competence to be one of the most sensitive parts of the business. Doing it well is important to the well-being of the client and the success of your business.

Former Clients
Former clients often still want to keep in touch. Friendships will develop with clients and continuing to maintain relationships with them and their family members is understandable. For a long-term client, her or his relationship with you on a day-to-day basis may be closer than that of anyone else during that time period.

When a Client Dies
The aging process makes us all more conscious of death and the mechanics of who does what when it happens. Death becomes more of a reality to seniors because they have undoubtedly lost a spouse, partner, family member, or friends. This subject is often the topic of

conversation among groups of seniors who are friends. A client will probably even talk to the concierge service provider about it. One of our clients unceremoniously handed my husband paperwork with details of her plan on how we and her family should handle things, which funeral home to call and what to do. Her husband had died at home and she knew all about the process. It was a calm and unemotional conversation. Not all clients are so pragmatic. It is important that you listen and make notes.

Additionally, you should create a short document for internal business use which outlines actions to take and information about contacts to be made by you and your company's service provider. When someone dies and you are the one who makes the discovery, it can be a shock and knowing what to do next helps. Having an existing relationship with the family representative is very valuable for your business and for the local authorities.

CHAPTER 5
SKILLS OF SERVICE PROVIDERS

We chose to be the service providers in our senior services business. This is because we wanted a part-time small business to fit in with our other businesses and still have our personal time. Additionally, we had gained an understanding of the needs of seniors and my husband had the personality to work with them in a very special way. It was a good fit.

The reality of this type of service is that the best way in the beginning for the owner(s) to gain the biggest financial benefit is to perform the work. This allows them to retain all the net income. As a business grows and has a larger number of clients, the work can be organized; service providers scheduled, and follow up procedures put in place.

The skills needed for both the owner(s) and service providers include:

- ❖ Respect for seniors and an interest in caring for them in a kind, caring, not domineering but firm manner

  If the person doesn't have this basic quality, she or he should not be placed in the homes and lives of your clients. Find someone else to represent your business.

- ❖ A clear understanding that the health and welfare of human beings is involved
- ❖ Patience
- ❖ Dependability (it is not OK to skip appointments or make changes without communicating with the client)
- ❖ Honesty
- ❖ Language skills-written and spoken
- ❖ Ability to converse easily in the language of the client.
- ❖ Organizational abilities

REMEMBER

Statistically women outlive men by 7-10 years. This increases the chances that your clients will be women. Some women will see your service as a comfort and feel more secure when learning to live alone. It may take them a year or so to adjust and gain confidences in their new routine.

Men who are widowed, or alone for other reasons, don't always seem as comfortable with a concierge service. Maybe it is because there are more single women than men <u>and</u> women are more comfortable reaching out to help others. You may find a man will accept a concierge service because it is a decision by his family and not because he is seeking it out.

Women who live alone often spend a lot of time with other women. We found that these women clients related better to a male as the service provider. They were quite honest in saying they appreciated a male presence in their daily lives.

- ❖ Follow-up
- ❖ Ability to respect the confidentiality of information about the client and her or his care Active listening skills
- ❖ Negotiation skills
- ❖ Willingness to avoid conflict with the client unless it involves life threatening situations
- ❖ Willing to be open-minded about the opinions, ideas, political, and religious beliefs of the client
- ❖ Adept at avoiding being involved or taking sides in family disagreements or conflicts
- ❖ Recognition that this is a business and on occasion this means setting boundaries with the client and his or her family

These qualities are found in people who enjoy helping others. Nurses, teachers, social workers, community volunteers, and those who give time and expertise in their faith communities are good candidates for this type of work.

Being a part-time service provider with a concierge service is a great way for a younger retiree to earn some extra income and be of service to others. After living around so many retirees, we noticed the younger ones sometimes just get bored. This is especially true if they're used to receiving a lot of emotional reward from their work.

Some people may already be good at working with seniors because they help family members, neighbors, or friends. You have to show them the value of their talents and experience. When trying to recruit a person to take over our remaining clients before we moved out of the area, my husband explained to a couple of people how our senior services business worked. One man, who spends a lot of time with the elderly, at his church told us "Well I do all of that already. The difference is I do it for free". He turned out to be a wonderful choice to work with our clients when we left.

You will develop your own list of qualities, talents, skills, and abilities to meet the needs of your clientele and the local area. However, the list provided is a great place to start.

CHAPTER 6
HOW TO MARKET

Marketing is simple and affordable. Referral business is the goal. To get there and stay there you will need some basic tools.

We used business cards, a brochure created in MS Word and printed from our personal computer, and a website with blog and static page capability. Later in the process we discovered that inexpensive business card magnets for the fridge were useful.

Printed Materials
Our business cards were ordered from www.printsmadeeasy.com and more recently from www.vistaprint.com. Just pick a template and put in your business information, including your website address. No need for a fancy logo and the expense which goes with it. Seniors and their families just want something nice, neat, colorful and EASY TO READ. Wherever possible, use large lettering in your materials.

The brochure information can be found on page 14.

Using the Internet
We used www.wordpress.com to host our blog website. In the past we have successfully used www.networksolutions.com for larger more complicated sites. We didn't feel we needed the expense. Wordpress.com is simpler to learn than the Network Solutions option.

The Wordpress platform is basically a blogging one with the capacity to add static pages. The only cost we incurred was $18 and that cost was for the domain name (___seniorservices.com) and to have the domain name linked to our wordpress.com site. We found the blogging capability to be very useful since it gave a place to make timely postings about our business activities and to share information about caring for seniors. Be advised that Wordpress sells advertising to companies and you may end up with some advertising on your site. If you wish, you can pay extra to avoid this situation. It never was a problem for us.

The target audience for the website is not the seniors who may become your clients; it is their families and others who are responsible for them. This is a way to show adult children that your company is professional and legitimate. You can share with them some things about working with seniors through informational postings. Most adult children living far away from parents are clueless. You will be teaching them.

The most important feature is how the website fits into your marketing plan. It is much easier, faster, and cheaper to email a link to your site (or give it to someone over the phone) than it is to mail a brochure and business card. The family can learn about potential costs, services, and gain information about you and your company. This is very useful when family members may not be able to meet you in person.

One of the things we learned was to use www.scribd.com which is a publishing website. This is a good way to include documents you wish to share (for example the information about service fees) on your website by publishing them on scribd.com and providing a link. You can learn more at www.scribd.com . Be certain your mark your documents as public so they can be accessed from your website.

Below is a list of organizations and companies you should consider contacting to let them know who you are and what you do. Be clear that you have a business and not a non-for-profit with independent financing. Be certain they understand you do not offer a service covered by Medicare, Medicaid, or health insurance. However, people employed in medical professions where they work and interact with seniors are usually extremely caring and they often are asked about whom to contact for a variety of services. We found it to be an informal yet important referral system.

- Social service agencies
- Home health care agencies
- Senior centers
- Medical clinics
- Religious centers (be sure to let the front office staff or leaders know about your business)
- Physical and occupational therapists who make house calls
- Retirement communities (you may find clients living there and often the staff members will meet seniors who chose not to reside in the retirement community but still need a little help)

Clearly, the most wonderful and effective way of marketing is the one where others do it for you. If you become known in communities of seniors and gain a good reputation, they will talk about your business over breakfast, at lunch, on the golf course, at the pool, in the aisles at Wal-Mart, at the beauty salon, and everywhere else. If a senior is one who doesn't go out a lot, don't worry. She or he too will learn about you when a friend comes to visit and brings all the latest news into the home. Faster than high school gossip for sure!

Business cards, a blog website, a simple brochure, networking, and reaching out to people who are seniors made up our marketing activities. The cost was nominal and the results were good. You will need to adapt, change, and supplement your marketing efforts to meet the needs of your locale and the seniors living there.

HOW TO MARKET
EXAMPLE OF INFORMATION FOR BASIC BROCHURE

Note: Use large font. Make another sheet with company information. Print a two sided brochure on colored paper and fold down the middle for an easy and affordable marketing tool to supplement your blog/website.

The Need for A Concierge

Does the senior in your life need to have something accomplished but doesn't have the time, no longer has the energy, or maybe has a physical limitation and can't do things like he or she used to?

Are you too far away to help? Does your schedule keep you from doing things for her or him? It may be something little like going to the grocery store, or a fun activity like planning and hosting a birthday party for his or her best friend.

A personal concierge service can help by taking care of things efficiently and easily for a fee.

Now is the time to consider ___ Senior Services as your choice for helping the senior in your life to remain as independent as possible.

Serving the area of xxx, xxx, xxx, and xxx.

Phone: _____
Email: _____
Website: _____

Some of the services we can provide are listed. All programs are personalized based on the needs of the senior.

What We Do for Seniors

Home helper services and errands
Provide medication reminders
Pick up prescriptions
Assist with laundry
Change linens
Assist with planning and preparing menus
Arrange appointments
Take out garbage
Write letters and correspondence
Ensure appointments are met
Organize and clean closets and cabinets
Escort to religious services
Assist with pet care
Shop for groceries
Care for plants
Conversation and companionship
Respite care for caregivers
Provide reminders for appointments
Mail bills and letters
Make plane reservations
Maintain calendar
Supervise home maintenance and interact with contractors
Monitor diet and exercise
Check food expirations
Assist with evening/morning routines
Maintain records of life events
Establish automatic bill paying or assist with submitting payments
Reconcile bank statements
Monitor insurance bills and payments

CHAPTER 7
LEGAL ISSUES

As stated in the introduction, there are a range of legal issues which need to be considered based on your individual business model along with potential requirements of your city, county, state and the federal government. For example, we made a decision not to offer transportation in our vehicles. The client provided the vehicle and we simply drove her or him, usually to medical appointments. It worked well because there was no requirement in our area for a driver in this situation to have a chauffer's license. That is not the case everywhere.

We were working in a small community with a very high need for our services. The client was motivated to have care "right now" and the families were supportive and relieved. You should seek legal guidance as you finalize your agreements and policies. If you find some major legal concerns you may want to adjust your agreements to be certain the client and the family representative work with you to understand both the <u>benefits</u> (significant) and <u>risks</u> (minor) involved in your service.

If we had chosen to expand and build a large clientele, we would have purchased the appropriate liability insurance and considered purchasing a vehicle for business purposes along with the appropriate insurance. This increases the cost of doing business and it wasn't needed for what we were doing.

We did not have any legal matters arise during the 3 years we were working with clients, but it could happen. The clients and family members usually see this as an interim arrangement. Both are usually more concerned about the client's immediate ability to handle day-to-day living and see the concierge's assistance as a major improvement over the current situation in terms of safety and comfort.

Additionally, working on a referral basis brings clients to you who are already more open and trusting. We had spent a couple of years caring for my family members and everybody knew who we were and how we conducted ourselves. We also knew a lot of seniors from our faith community. Starting from a position of trust with anyone helps a lot. With older people it is just huge and they transfer that confidence to family members. Interestingly, seniors are still competitive about things and they may see your service as a perk their friend has and one that they need.

To summarize, know your clients, do what you promise, and seek some basic legal advice before you start. As things evolve the legal issues will probably become more significant, but that is true of any business as it becomes more profitable. If you find a client or a family to be more wrapped up in the legalities of every situation, it could be a sign of things to come and you may want to decline offering them services. It is your business!

CHAPTER 8
BUSINESS PRACTICES
PRIVACY OF CLIENT INFORMATION

Your senior service business, and those involved with it, will occasionally have access to private information about clients. For example, picking up prescriptions at the local pharmacy usually involves providing the patient's name and date of birth. Often the service provider will help the client with requests for information that require disclosing insurance information. It is difficult to help the client without being able to communicate with others who are authorized by the client to have the information.

As with any business, the control of private information is important. Information may be printed documents, but includes anything about the client which is personal and private. It is very important that service providers remain discreet and not share any personal information with anyone other than the authorized family representative. Seniors share information and some even gossip among themselves. You, your service providers, and your company should not be involved in creating or adding to these exchanges of information. The client deserves respect and to be treated with dignity.

Be sure to shred documents which contain personal information. It shouldn't be much of a problem because the level of paperwork in the business is limited. Just be aware of the obligation you have to the client to guard his or her privacy. There are a variety of resources available concerning identity theft prevention. If this is a practice you haven't had to use before, now is a good time to learn.

It is not difficult to avoid security problems. It takes a little common sense, a shredder from the local store, and an understanding that emailing or verbally sharing private information about clients is not acceptable,

BUSINESS PRACTICES
VISIT LOGS AND ACCOUNTABILITY

Keeping records is important for a variety of reasons.

- ❖ First, they tell the story of your interactions with the client. This can be shared with the client or the family representative in the event of a service question or concern. They help validate your version of services provided.

- ❖ Next, these records help you to periodically evaluate the time spent with your client to ensure the fees charged are appropriate. You can increase or decrease fees easier if there is data to support the change.

- ❖ The records can also help you evaluate whether or not a client's needs have shifted radically. This is when a collaborative decision among the client, family representative, and you will be needed.

- ❖ Logs and accountability are even more important when using service providers who work for you as independent contractors or employees. In addition to written records, you should consider using a system similar to one we learned by observing home health care providers. The service provider is part of a dispatch system which requires calling, texting, or sending data via a smart phone to the office. A simple version of this would be to have your service provider text or call you upon completion of the client visit or activity. This helps avoid service problems such as missed calls, late arrivals, or a failure to report significant changes in the client's situation.

A log can be easily created in word processing and printed in the landscape setting. Each client has different needs, but an example of some of the activities to include in a log follows:

Client Name									
Date	**Start/Stop Time**	**Trash**	**Mail**	**Shopping**	**House Clean/Maint.**	**Drs.Appt**	**Paperwork**	**Car/Cart**	**Other**

BUSINESS PRACTICES
EXAMPLE OF AGREEMENT WITH FAMILY REPRESENTATIVE DESIGNATION AND PERMISSION

____ SENIOR SERVICES
Authorization for Services

This Services Agreement is made and entered into this _____ day of _____, ____, by and between _____ _____ (client), an individual residing at _____, and ____Senior Services (Company), having offices at _____

1. Throughout the period of this agreement, ___ Senior Services will provide the services listed below for the Client. Client, or their assigned party, will be advised of the status of the services.

2. The services to be provided include, but are not limited to:

   Drive client to appointments in local ___ mile radius to towns of xxx & xxx (1 per month)
   Hurricane preparation and transportation of self and vehicle to safe area away from _____I
   Organize medications weekly
   Help organize or clean closets
   Provide appointment reminders
   Resolve minor computer issue.
   Routine household chores (empty trash etc.) other than cleaning.
   Daily contact/check-in. (six home visits, one phone check-in weekly)
   Shop as requested
   Handle visitor transportation
   Coordinate car care
   Be an advocate for insurance and other financial issues

   Other duties as discussed.
   _____

3. For services rendered under this Agreement, the client will pay the Company, upon presentation of its invoice a fee _____per month due at the beginning of the service period and non-refundable.

4. The client, or the company, may terminate the services of the Company at the end of any service month in writing or by declaration to the company.

5. The following individual is designated as my family representative:

   Name: _____

   Address: _____

   Phone: _____

   Email: _____

   I understand that a representative of _____Senior Services has authority to contact my family representative and share information about my care, well-being, and other personal matters.

Client Signature _____   Date_____

____ Senior Services by _____   Date _____

BUSINESS PRACTICES
EXAMPLE OF LETTER WHEN FAMILY MEMBER INITIATES SERVICE REQUEST

Dear Family Representative:

My wife and I met with your mother, xxxxxx xxxxx, this morning and had a very enjoyable and informative meeting. I'll make this a short narrative of our conversation and those tasks she feels she needs to have done, so she can stay in her home here in xxx versus moving into a retirement community or assisted living.

She readily admits that she has slowed down significantly over the past two years and that her friends and neighbors, although having been very helpful, have also slowed down, and that they want to step back from doing many of the day-to-day tasks that your mother still needs to have someone perform.

She said that she needs someone to do the following tasks:

1. Cleaning her home
2. Grocery shopping
3. Doing her laundry
4. Changing the bed linens.
5. Picking up medication, as needed
6. Taking her to doctor's appointments, as needed
7. Picking up her mail.

She still seems to be fairly sharp, and appears to have a good memory compared to many of her contemporaries down here, but physically, she has slowed down quite a bit. We know from experience that daily contact gives a better picture of what is really going on. Based on what she told us, she stays at home, prepares her own meals, does not drive, and does not participate in social events. Her contacts are with neighbors and family visits. She finds this routine comfortable and clearly feels this lifestyle works for her. She states that she takes care of her own bills with the majority of them being EFT from her account. At this time she does not have a life alert system since she depends on the neighbors.

I would make the following proposal. ___ Senior Services would:
1. Check in with your mother on a daily basis and get her mail for her and mail any letters/bills
2. Pick up her laundry and change out her linens on a weekly basis, and wash these items.
3. Take out her garbage on a regular basis.

4. Go grocery shopping on a weekly basis for her, per her grocery list. (She stated that she still cooks and likes to prepare her own meals. We would monitor this to insure she is eating properly}.
5. Hire a housekeeper to clean her home every two weeks by an individual we currently work with. We will monitor the scheduling and your mother will pay the housekeeper.
6. Drive her to doctor's appointments within the local area and to xxx and xxx.). She currently has friends accompanying her on these appointments and act as medical "buddies". We can perform that duty also. (At this point, we're estimating a maximum of one appointment per month. She feels that it is less than this. Should we find that we have more appointments than that, we may need to make an adjustment in the monthly rate).
7. Pick up her medications from the pharmacist, as needed.
8. Assist and coordinate with maintenance/repairmen to insure that she is getting treated fairly.

We would also communicate with the designated family member concerning any changes we observe or concerns she expresses.

For services rendered under this Agreement, the client will pay the Company, upon presentation of its invoice a fee of _____. We require payment in advance. The reasons for this are explained on our website.

The client, or the company, may terminate the services of the Company at the end of any service month in writing or by declaration to the company.

In addition to the option of having us provide services, we talked about a retirement community in xxx as an option. We even suggested she visit one we have toured.

I told her that we would be talking to you, and I would be providing periodic reports.

Please give me a call or email me, with any questions or concerns.

I look forward to a long and mutually beneficial business relationship.

Sincerely,

Owner
___Senior Services
Phone:
Email:
Website

CHAPTER 9
CLOSING THE DEAL

The Deal

Our agreement with the client required a <u>monthly</u> service with a <u>non-refundable payment in advance</u>. Additionally, for services provided which were outside the scope of the agreement, payment was required at the completion of the service. For example, sometimes the number of trips out of the local area exceeded the allowed trips on the contract. So the cost for that trip was collected when the client arrived at home.

My husband learned during his management consulting days that selling an intangible is different from selling a product. Prompt payment is <u>very</u> important. A concierge also provides an intangible service and that makes it difficult to collect from the client who chooses not to pay. If you sell someone a TV or a couch, you can take it back. As a concierge, once you have provided service to the client, there is no easy way to recoup payment. Seniors may often have different memories of what they promised and aging can affect memory and moods. If they end up in the hospital or experience some other serious change in their routines, you may not get paid. This puts you in the position of negotiating with the family representative for payment. We were able to skip all these issues by requiring payment in advance.

Our services were available only to clients who were on a monthly agreement. This was a good decision. People will opt not to have your monthly service in an attempt to save money. They will then call when they are having some type of problem. They will also assume that you will be available to them whenever they wish. It is hard to make money consistently if you are relying on a bunch of individual sporadic service requests. Having the monthly agreement allowed us to have a more predictable cash flow and schedule our work to accommodate both the daily routines of our clients, and also the unexpected things which happen during emergencies such as illness or hurricane evacuation. You will find that your clients will recognize not everyone has the privilege of your time and talents. This gives them positive reinforcement that becoming a client of your company was a good decision.

It may sound pushy or rather cold hearted, to collect in advance but it worked well for us and the clients. Once the client saw the value of the service received, writing that monthly check was easy and a great reminder to continue to use the service.

Closing the Deal

In every business, the sales process is just as important as creating a good service, selecting the appropriate staff members marketing, and providing a quality service. People who work in businesses or career fields involved in caring for people tend not to have any experience in actually getting the client to sign a contract and collecting a payment. This chapter can help make closing the deal a little easier.

The word "sales "creates a lot of strong and often negative emotions for many people. Please remember, sales is not about forcing people to buy something they don't want, it is really about giving the client what she or he needs. Sales and closing "the deal" are not some difficult high pressure tactics to force a client into your business. It is a mutually beneficial situation. If it isn't, then you don't have the right potential client.

> The only way a person can benefit from your service is if she or he purchases it.
>
> If you have been invited to the home to talk about your service that is a big step for the senior.
>
> Remember, you may represent the best opportunity for a senior to remain in his or her home or to continue a current living arrangement.

Let's assume you have used a marketing process like the one described in this guide and it is now time to have the client sign on the dotted line and start receiving your services. There are some basic concepts which can help and make you more successful.

- ❖ **Be confident about what you offer**. If the client is truly a good fit for your business, it will improve her or his life. With seniors there can be real threats to their safety and security if they are living alone without any consistent and reliable outside assistance. Please use this as your motivation when it comes time for them to sign a contract. Most will hesitate a little, but some will be excited and appreciative.

- ❖ **Explain the cost.** This is the usual sticking point with seniors. As a financial advisor I had learned to show people how the solution I was proposing improved their lives as an alternative to the current situation. In the case of a senior, mention how cost effective your services are compared to other alternatives such as re-locating to a fulltime living facility. Ask them what they will have to give up in order to pay you. Often seniors who are considering a concierge service used to take trips, go on cruises, spend money on shopping and gifts, or basically indulge in consumer spending. As they age this shifts and these activities may become difficult or impossible to enjoy. So, the money they are saving by that lifestyle change can be channeled into the concierge service cost and become their new lifestyle.   Many seniors tend to want to hang on to their money yet still be taken care of by others. It is a version of having their cake and eating it too. You may need to gently remind them that their financial resources are really there to support their needs first and it is O.K. to spend money to have assistance which helps them live more safely and securely. It is also OK to accept a gift of service paid by concerned family members or others.

- **Understand how to overcome the client's fear of making a commitment.** Making a long term commitment is hard for most people and can be even more difficult for seniors. This is the value of a monthly contract. If the client choses to terminate the relationship, it is an easy process. However, if a client terminates the agreement and wants to return, there may not be a space available for her or him. We had that happen once and it didn't seem to occur to the client that availability was limited. Additionally, you as the service provider have the option to terminate the agreement after completing the service month. This balance of power with both parties works very well.

- **Ask for the client's signature on the agreement and pick up the first payment**. After you have given the client all the information available, ask for the sale.   Simply go over the agreement and ask him or her to sign. If the client seems uncomfortable or confused, go over the client's concerns. If you still find the client is not ready to sign, it is time to walk away. Let the client know they may call you again, but you take a limited number of clients and there may not be an available opening when they need it.   It often helps to have a motivated family representative involved in the agreement signing and payment process.

CHAPTER 10
MAKING MONEY
PRICING, INCOME, AND EXPENSES

This is an internal planning document to help support the monthly fee calculation for the service agreement. You will need to determine whether to charge the client for travel time to and from his or her home. Additionally, there may be other costs to consider which the client will need to pay another provider directly. For example, you may chose not to perform home cleaning and the cost for that would be paid directly by the client to the housekeeper. The challenge is to balance out the overall fee to make it reasonable yet financially worthwhile to you or your business. Fees vary according to the cost of living in different areas, but be realistic about what you charge.

_____ **Senior Services**

Example of Weekly Estimate Worksheet

<u>Home Helper Services</u>   - $ _____ per hour.

- ☐ Pick up Rx, groceries, cleaning, run errands _____
- ☐ Change linens _____
- ☐ Assist with planning menus _____
- ☐ Assist with preparing meals _____
- ☐ Arrange Appointments _____
- ☐ Take out garbage _____
- ☐ Write letters or correspondence _____
- ☐ Drive to appointments _____
- ☐ Accompany to lunch or dinner _____
- ☐ Organize and clean cabinets and closets _____
- ☐ Escort to religious services _____
- ☐ Assist with pet care _____
- ☐ Other _____

<u>Financial Services</u> - _____ per hour, or as stated
- ☐ Pay bills _____
- ☐ Bank Reconciliation $20.00 per month per account
- ☐ Insurance Advocacy or Billing _____
- ☐ Other _____

<u>Companionship Services</u> - $_____ per hour
- ☐ Companionship or respite care _____
- ☐ Mail bills and letters _____
- ☐ Maintain calendar _____

_____ **Senior Services**

Monthly Estimate Worksheet (Cont.)

- ☐ Monitor diet and exercise _____
- ☐ Check food expirations _____
- ☐ Supervise home maintenance _____
- ☐ Assist with entertaining _____
- ☐ Assist with evening / morning routines _____
- ☐ Other _____

Home Helper Services _____hrs/wk. X $ _____ = _____

Financial Services _____hrs/wk. X $ _____ = _____

Bank Reconciliation _____each X _____ = _____

Companionship Services _____hrs/wk. X _____ = _____

Estimated Dollar Total/Week   _____

Client _____

Company Representative _____ Date _____

There are costs to consider and include in determining an hourly rate. If you are an experienced business person or cost analyst, this section will seem simple and unnecessary. However, this may be your first experience in creating a service business it may feel a little overwhelming. So this section will get you started. Things to consider include:

- ❖ Local hourly costs of comparable of service providers. This can be difficult to determine but you can search the Internet for website of concierges and senior services providers to get an idea.

- ❖ Business expenses such as marketing, transportation costs, taxes, technology, telecommunications, legal, rent (if needed), and internet service providers. These should be considered when determining base hourly rates

- ❖ Adjust your pricing based on a comparison of the cost of living for your locale versus theirs. We used a baseline of $25 per hour with a half hour minimum per service activity for our area. However, in a larger more affluent area, the client may be willing to pay more. Similarly, in other areas the cost of living may be significantly less and the client will accordingly pay less. A lot of it depends on the labor cost in your area or, if you are performing the work yourself, the minimum net income you are willing to accept.

The more clients you work with over time, the more skilled you will become at meeting the clients' needs and making the cost fair for you and them. As mentioned earlier, the agreement is on a month-to-month basis. If you misjudge the client's needs, you can do a review after the first month and increase or decrease the cost as needed. If the client doesn't agree, either one of you can terminate the contract. So, we always felt that the worst that could happen is we might take a small loss for one month. We tried very hard not to change agreement prices unless the client's needs changed. It is just upsetting to her or his routine.

CHAPTER 11
BLOG WEBSITE WITH STATIC PAGES

We found the combined approach of having a blog website with static pages to work well. The blog allowed us to easily post writings, pictures, and links to articles of interest about topics pertaining to seniors. It is easy to find good articles and videos which educate others about the issues faced by seniors. This is a service to your viewers. A blog also allows for a dialog with others interested in the care of seniors. Learning is a sharing experience.

Although you won't see the tags on the following pages, we always made certain to include our city and the surrounding cities as tags on each posting. This, combined with tags identifying the topics for each posting, helps attract views to your site. The idea is to have your website viewed by family members outside your local area who are looking for a concierge service (hopefully yours) in your area. The static pages require very little maintenance, but can be easily changed to accommodate updates for things like contact information, fee changes, and other administrative items.

The following pages were taken from our website. You will see that our local weather threat was hurricanes. You can adapt the information you provide to reflect possible emergency situations which occur where you live. These may be extended snow/ice storms, floods, tornadoes, etc. These pages are provided to encourage you to create your own site which reflects your local community and the needs of seniors where you live.

CHAPTER 11
BLOG WEBSITE WITH STATIC PAGES

_____ Senior Services

Serving the areas of xxx, xxx, xxx, and xxx
TABS FOR STATIC PAGES

- **About**
- **About-What We Do for Seniors**
- **Frequently Asked Questions**
- **Service Fees**

BLOG POSTINGS
How to talk to seniors about moving from home into senior-living

Click here to watch some very helpful videos about helping seniors make the change from living at home to senior living. Lots of very meaningful information for friends and families of seniors!

Leave a Comment » | ℰ | Tagged: Aging and changes, How to and senior living, Retirement Living, Senior Living | Permalink
Posted by Debra

Great article

Please go to http://www.scribd.com/doc/52005401/churchservingfinalpdf to read an article about how families are coping with seniors who are geographically separated from them. Having encountered the same situation, Terry was inspired to create _____ Senior Services for the area of xxx, xxx, xxx and xxx. Great article !!
Leave a Comment » | ℰ, | Permalink
Posted by Debra

Holiday Celebrations!

Best Wishes to all for this wonderful holiday celebration. We are pleased to have delivered home-made banana bread to our clients. A joy for us and a treat to share with them.

Leave a Comment » |, Uncategorized | Tagged: Christmas, ___ Senior Services | Permalink
Posted by Debra

Easter Wishes

Best wishes for a Blessed Easter. These are some of the Easter baskets we delivered to our clients. Fun things for us, and hopefully for them. It will probably be the first Easter basket which is in a bag and has a Mango!

Leave a Comment » | Permalink
Posted by Debra

Great info!

Want to learn more about the benefit of using computers and moderate exercise for seniors? Just Click here

Leave a Comment » | | Tagged: aging, cognitive retention, mental health | Permalink
Posted by Debra

Great info on ABC News

This week Diane Sawyer, ABC News, has been doing a series on seniors, elderly, and their families. You can learn more at the ABC News website. The segment about the "driving" question is particularly useful. Just click here to view it.

Leave a Comment » | Seniors | Tagged: ABC News, elderly driving, elderly safety | Permalink
Posted by Debra

The "driving" conversation

A great article about driving and seniors. Just highlight and click on the previous sentence (the one in purple) and it will take you to it. Enjoy

Leave a Comment » | Seniors | Tagged: driving safety, seniors driving auto | Permalink
Posted by Debra

Funniest video from a senior

One of our friends who is a nurse sent us this link. It is the best! The speaker is a 72 year old woman and she conveys the aging story with class, humor and understanding. Worth watching!

http://www.caregiverstress.com/2010/07/a-reminder-that-laughter-is-the-best-medicine/
Leave a Comment » | | Tagged: aging, humor, senior care | Permalink
Posted by Debra

Making print large on computer screens

This is an interesting article about how to easily improve the ease of reading text on the computer screen, something which is frustrating for many!

Leave a Comment » | Seniors, Uncategorized | Tagged: computers and seniors, reading computers | Permalink
Posted by Debra

Need help with your computer?

One of the things we have experienced is that sometimes using technology seems to become more challenging as people age. If everything works fine, then all is well. A small thing to us at ____ Senior Services can be a big thing to our customer who is left wondering what to do. So, when there is a problem, like the printer doesn't work correctly, or email doesn't operate the way it used to, we can help.

Recently we assisted a customer with selecting a new desktop computer and did what was needed to remove vital information from the old computer and to hook up the new one and showing the customer how it works.

The next part of the process concerns what to do with old computers and their monitors when no longer needed. These items shouldn't be put in the trash. We suggest finding a recycling program like the one at Best Buy . We can coordinate this for our customers.

If you need this type of assistance, please email us at ____ or call ____

Leave a Comment » | , Seniors, , Uncategorized | Tagged: Best Buy, computers | Permalink
Posted by Debra

New page added

We have included more detailed information about ___ Senior Services to help you and the senior in your life better understand some of the things we offer. Please see the page called" What We Do for Seniors"

Leave a Comment » | | Tagged: concierge, errands, financial management, senior companion | Permalink
Posted by Debra

What is diminished capacity?

From Debra Hadsall

I realize this isn't a popular term or concept. The two words– **diminished** and **capacity**– bring up a lot of emotional responses. So let's take a moment to look at some characteristics of what you might be seeing in the seniors in your life. While these characteristics do not necessarily pertain only to those who are seniors, they are things which tend to happen as part of the aging process.

Some characteristics of diminished capacity are: memory loss, repetition in speech, disorientation, mood swings, and difficulty in processing basic information.

Medical professionals are best trained to help you understand how to work with a person exhibiting these characteristics. However, there are a few administrative procedures and communication tools you can use to decrease the confusion and frustration by all involved.

First, it may be time to start creating a written record of agreements and events concerning the senior. When important meetings are held about finances, medical care, and household matters, a meeting summary will prove useful to ensure everyone understands the process and the outcome. A medical buddy might be the best choice for someone who has frequent appointments with doctors. Finally, when making decisions with, or on behalf of the senior, the family member can prepare a written summary of the process to be certain that there is a record to rely on, rather than counting on someone to remember. You may feel uncomfortable making notes and keeping records of things which seem to be routine. A few weeks, months, or even years later you will be glad you did.

These are just a few characteristics of diminished capacity and some basic tools to help you to start to manage the situation and to help both you and the senior. We also find that a sense of adventure combined with a humorous approach to non-life threatening situations can be a big help.

We at ____ Senior Services can help by providing concierge services for your family members who may be experiencing characteristics of diminished capacity and just need a little help, organization, and assistance to maintain a reasonable level of personal independence.

Leave a Comment » | | Tagged: aging, concierge, diminished capacity, senior services, | Permalink
Posted by Debra

Being Prepared-Hurricanes and Other Events

Being Prepared…Makes Sense

I have been attending informational meetings provided by the local government and planning authorities. Thought I would share what I learned. If you haven't accomplished all these things, don't know where to start, or need some help getting organized, these are things we can do for our clients at ____LRGV Senior Services.

Preparing for emergencies before they happen makes sense.

Whatever the summer season brings, whether it's a tropical storm, tornado, or hurricane, there are things we can do to make sure we are ready.

Evaluating your own personal needs and making a plan that fits those needs, you and your loved ones can be better prepared.

Get a Kit Of Emergency Supplies. These are Basic Supplies: food, water, any life-sustaining items you require.

Make a Plan for what you will do in an Emergency

Remember that you will likely not have access to everyday conveniences in a disaster situation. Think through the details of your everyday life and the people who assist you. Create a personal plan, write it down and share with your family and friends.

Be Informed about What Might Happen

It's important to stay informed about what might happen and how it will affect you.

Be prepared to adapt this information to your personal circumstances and follow the instructions received from the authorities.

For more information about Being Prepared…

National Hurricane Center: http://www.nhc.noaa.gov

American Red Cross: http://www.redcross.org

Federal Emergency Management Agency: http://www.fema.gov

Leave a Comment » | , Seniors, Uncategorized | Tagged: Hurricane, | Permalink
Posted by Debra

What is a concierge service?

Did you ever need to have something done but you don't have the time, no longer have the energy, or maybe you have a physical limitation and just can't do it yourself? It may be something little like going to the grocery store, or something more fun like planning and hosting a birthday party for your best friend. A personal concierge service can help. You pay someone to take care of things efficiently and easily.

Now is a good time to think about your "to do" list of things and to contact ____ Senior Services for help. We serve the area of xxx, xxx, xxx, and xxx.

Please call us at ____ or email ____ for more information about our fees, services, and gift certificates.

2 Comments | Seniors, Uncategorized | Tagged: aging, assistant, concierge, errands, helper, independent living,, , mature adults, medical buddy, personal services, senior services, seniors, |
Permalink
Posted by Debra

Do my parents need help?

It's a difficult decision but one many of us face. Do my parents need help? How can I tell if my parents are OK living alone? This article will help you.

Leave a Comment » | Seniors, Uncategorized | Tagged: aging, assistant, , concierge, errands, helper, independent living, , mature adults, medical buddy, personal services, senior services, seniors, , | Permalink
Posted by Debra

BLOG WEBSITE WITH STATIC PAGES
EXAMPLES OF STATIC PAGES

ABOUT

After living in the local area for three years and being involved in the local community, (owner's name) recognized the need for concierge services for seniors. The xxxx area is a resort and retirement community. As a result there is a concentration of mature adults who quite often have few or no family members in the local area.
____Senior Services can step in to offer services needed by individuals to maintain independence. We support both the client and the client's family.

____ Senior Services

Email: ____

Phone: ____

PHOTO OF OWNER, PRESIDENT, PRINCIPALS

BLOG WEBSITE WITH STATIC PAGES
EXAMPLES OF STATIC PAGES

ABOUT US
The Need for A Concierge

Does the senior in your life need to have something accomplished but doesn't have the time, no longer has the energy, or maybe has a physical limitation and can't do things like he or she used to?

Are you too far away to help? Does your schedule keep you from doing things for them? It may be something little like going to the grocery store, or a fun activity fun like planning and hosting a birthday party for his or her best friend.

A personal concierge service can help by taking care of things efficiently and easily for a fee.

Now is the time to consider ___Senior Services as your choice for helping the senior in your life to remain as independent as possible.

Serving the area of xxx, xxx, xxx, and xxx.

Phone:___
Email: ____
Website____

Some of the services we can provide are listed. All programs are personalized based on the needs of the senior.

What We Do for Seniors

Home helper services and errands
Provide medication reminders
Pick up prescriptions
Assist with laundry
Change linens
Assist with planning, preparing menus
Arrange appointments
Take out garbage
Write letters and correspondence
Ensure appointments are met
Organize and clean closets and cabinets
Accompany to lunch or dinner or events
Assist with pet care
Shop for groceries
Care for plants
Conversation and companionship
Respite care for caregivers
Provide reminders for appointments
Mail bills and letters
Plan visits, outings and trips
Make plane reservations
Maintain calendar
Supervise home maintenance and interact with contractors
Monitor diet and exercise
Check food expirations
Assist with evening/morning routines
Maintain records of life events
Establish automatic bill paying or assist with submitting payments
Reconcile bank statements
Monitor insurance bills and payments

My To Do List

As you think of things you need to do or have done, please use this form to list them. It will help us to better understand your needs and see how to serve you best.

Thanks

Owner Name

Company Name, Address
Email: Phone:

_____

_____

_____

_____

_____

_____

_____

_____

_____

BLOG WEBSITE WITH STATIC PAGES
EXAMPLES OF STATIC PAGES

Service Fees

We are a concierge business offering a specialized service to families who have recognized that an older family member can no longer safely, easily, and comfortably live alone. We serve the local area of xxx, xxx, xxx, and xxx.

____Senior Services provides a high touch service that requires an understanding of the needs of the family members who may not be local, as well as the daily habits of the client who is a senior in the local area.

Our basic program offers 10 hours of service a month, with a half hour minimum for each call or activity. Our standard program increases the hours to 25 hours of service per month.

___Senior Services maintains a log of the time and services provided and allows one hour per month to rollover. If the hours exceed the program hours (10 or 25) hours per month plus the rollover hours, the family will be asked to evaluate the need for additional hours. As the needs of seniors vary based on health, schedules, and the weather (for example, the local area of xxx, has potential for hurricanes) and it is difficult to predict with accuracy the requirements for each month.

The agreement is offered on a month- to- month basis and is paid in advance. It may be renewed or cancelled at the beginning of each service month.

10 hours per month	$350
25 hours per month	$500

For more information, please refer to our frequently asked questions page.

BLOG WEBSITE WITH STATIC PAGES
EXAMPLES OF STATIC PAGES
FREQUENTLY ASKED QUESTIONS

____ Senior Services,
Serving the Areas of xxx, xxx, xxx, and xxx
www.___seniorservices.com

1. How does a concierge service differ from other senior services I see advertised for home care?

Home care usually refers to health care of varying levels. A concierge service is a program which is often described as a personal assistant, errand running, companionship services, and personal bookkeeping all coordinated through one person or business.

2. Why do you bill a month in advance?

The type of service we provide is very personalized and we want to ensure there is not a break in service which could disrupt the senior's schedule. Consistency of care and maintaining routines become more important as people age. Seniors are often reluctant to ask for assistance or rely on others, until something happens. By paying in advance the senior is encouraged to use the service and we are able to plan appropriately and commit our staff over the month. The types of services vary widely. We can easily coordinate a variety of activities, something which is difficult for the senior. We see ourselves as an extension of the family, to provide assistance in the absence of family members.

3. Will Medicare of Medicaid pay for a senior's monthly service?

There may a few instances where some of the services are authorized for payment by an insurance program, including Medicare. However, the client or the client's family will need to pay us and seek reimbursement from insurer. We do not submit billings to insurance companies.

4. What kind of things can I expect my senior to receive from the monthly concierge service?

Each person is different, but we have listed examples of services the page marked "What We Do for Seniors". Please just go to that page and review or print the list.

5. How many clients do you work with at a time? What assurance do I have that my senior's needs will be met?

We accept a limited number of clients at a time and offer the monthly programs only. This gives us the flexibility to ensure we can provide service during peak needs times, such as helping prepare for hurricane evacuation or helping the client with planning for a special occasion.

6. What are the alternatives to using a concierge?

Once again, each situation is different. However, the local area of xxx does not have a local hospital and has limited nursing care available. So the options include moving to be with family members elsewhere, relocating to one of the larger cities (_____) or other locations where there are retirement communities and assisted living and other care facilities. Over time one or all of these may become necessary, but often having a concierge service extends the time a senior can stay in his or her home.

7. Will you make a report to let me see each month's activities and time spent on them?

Yes. In addition to working with the senior, we require a family member be designated as the family representative and we furnish a periodic report to him or her. This is accomplished with the written approval of the senior. This way even though you aren't here locally, you can have an added perspective of the lifestyle and requirements of the senior.

8. If there is an emergency, will you contact me?

Yes, as mentioned earlier, we require contact information of the family representative who will be informed of emergencies as we become aware of them.

9. What can I do if I believe my senior needs this service but he or she won't purchase it?

This is pretty common. In the beginning it is difficult to convince anybody, especially seniors, to purchase something when he or she does not see a need. Often an outsider, like a concerned family member, can see things more clearly and recognize the value of our program. We offer gift certificates for our service agreements. A family member, or a group of family members, may want to purchase the first month's service to introduce the senior to the service. If the senior is not financially capable of paying for the program, but family members are, then a series of gift certificates are a solution.

10. Do you have references?

We can provide references upon request. You can learn about the owner on the "About "page of this website.

CHAPTER 12
A FEW MORE TIPS

This chapter is titled "A Few More Tips" and brings the guide to a close. These tips are based on our experiences. They cover the topics about being a resource connection, active listening and observing, dealing with the tricky issue of driving and seniors, and the value of a good sense of humor.

Over time you will probably develop your own tip sheet, but these are issues which turned out to be important to the success of our business. Best wishes and good luck as you create and sustain your own Concierge Service for Seniors.

As a concierge, you will be expected to know your way around the area you serve. It is important to have quick access to contact information about quality service providers who can assist your clients.

We kept a notebook with business cards placed in plastic sheets. This was our notebook to use for our clients. It has value and we generally didn't make referrals to non-clients or their families. If you give away the results of your networking, screening, and experience in finding good companies to work with, you have given away your income. It is not uncommon for family members who are geographically isolated from parents to try and manage things from afar, using free information from local experts (that would be you). In the introduction of this guide I stated that a concierge provides a service in return for payment, even though some customers prefer the service to be free. Something as intangible as a referral to a trusted local business may seem to be of no financial consequence to a client or family member, but that is not true. Once I spent three hours calling hotels in cities far enough away for us to take clients in the event of hurricane evacuation. I carefully confirmed the phone numbers, locations, restaurant capabilities, and other items important to seniors. This list then became as asset of our business to use with our clients. They knew about the information and our plans for them. They were appreciative and felt confident they would be cared for in the event of an evacuation. Evacuation for potential hurricanes may not be your concern, but it illustrates how support procedures you develop have value and should be treated as such.

Our business card notebook contained contact information about services such as:

- ❖ Home cleaning services
- ❖ Gardeners and lawn maintenance
- ❖ Plumbers
- ❖ Electricians
- ❖ Air conditioner and heating repair techs
- ❖ Carpet cleaners
- ❖ Hairstylists and nail care specialists (including those who make house calls)

- Attorneys
- Banks
- Furniture stores
- Car repair shops
- All types of mail and shipping services
- Computer repair techs
- Medical care providers and facilities
- Veterinarians
- Pharmacies
- Restaurants and places which will deliver food
- Internet and cable TV providers
- Laundry service or people who will wash/dry clothes
- Tax preparers
- Churches and places of worship
- Airport transportation
- Utility (electric and gas) companies
- Safety alert system companies

Actively listening and observing during interactions with clients is really important to their well-being and helps you to better meet their needs in a timely and organized manner.

The consistent and daily, or almost daily, contact with the client turned out to be a core component of the success of our senior services business. Human contact is important to the senior and the service provider. The client looks forward to the visit and it is important to be consistent in showing up on the day and time scheduled.

The service provider needs to be engaged with the client during visits. A few questions to show genuine concern are useful. We always asked how things were going and inquired about what the client had been doing since we last saw or talked to her or him. Our conversations might be about successes or challenges of family members, things going on with their friends, or something as seemingly harmless like a sleepless night or a change in health. This is the time to ask if there is something that needs to be accomplished to help. It may be something simple you can do, like buying a greeting card. Then it might turn out to be more drastic such as driving the client to the doctor or helping her or him learn to properly take a newly prescribed medicine.

Listening is a big deal! So is looking around the house to see if anything seems to be different or needing attention. For example, in one home our client's friend had placed a living plant at the top of a very tall bookcase. The client was going to get out the ladder and water the plant, an act which we discourage. So the service provider easily took care of it, the client was very happy, and all was well. Little things to a service provider are major tasks for seniors. Safety and security of the client is one of the benefits of your service. You, or your service provider, can help avoid most dangerous situations, if there is interaction with the client, active listening, careful observation, and timely action.

The tips about being a connection to resources and actively listening and observing when interacting with the client may just sound like common sense. However, to those of us who are functioning well in society, we may just assume the senior is operating at the same level that we are, just a little slower. That may not be the case, so rely more on your hands on experiences and less on assumptions of what her or his capabilities may be.

Educate yourself about the subject of seniors driving motor vehicles.

Driving a motor vehicle is a privilege and not a right. This concept gets lost over time and it can become really difficult for people who have driven for many years to understand that it is time to let someone else do the driving. Additionally, there is not much legal consensus about how to force someone to quit driving, unless it has to do with impairments from illegal substances and alcohol or a record of traffic related incidents.

Some organizations in the country have developed written materials and testing programs to help someone determine her or his driving capabilities. For example, the University of Michigan is a good resource for information about their SAFER program. Ask medical providers, especially those who work with the elderly, about local resources. Additionally, there are written guides which can be downloaded from the Internet. The challenge with these is that the senior does a self-assessment by answering questions. Often the senior's view of how she or he drives is not always a reflection of the truth. A more objective approach administered by a third party is optimal. As we moved to another part of the country we learned that the local hospital had developed a testing location and process. This is very exciting and hopefully more of these centers will open. Maybe you will want to research the business opportunity for a center and open one. The need is significant and growing.

Your concierge service can be part of the transportation and driving solution. You can encourage clients to carpool with friends who are competent drivers, show them how to call a taxi, and rely on your company when needed for longer or emergency trips. If you grocery shop for clients and pickup prescriptions, you have helped them decrease their driving times.

It is very difficult to "make" anyone, especially a senior with a car and money to pay for gas and insurance, to decide to give up driving. Some of the conversations we had with clients were not only about the safety and welfare of the client, but also the concern for others. Most seniors who have been relatively accident free through their driving lives can't actually visualize the paperwork nightmare and inconvenience caused by an accident. Some will feel they can live with the risk of being injured or killed. This is a normal risk everyone takes, but a driver who is suffering from diminished capacity due to age related cognitive and physical limitations puts others at risk.

Sometimes it helps to point out the legal liability involved in car accidents. Seniors with retirement income, property, investment accounts, and other assets may be putting it all at risk. They may or may not have legally protected themselves from the legal impact of an accident which occurs when they are driving. Most people didn't work hard and reach the later years of their lives to have their financial resources and lifestyles reduced. Framing it this way can be helpful.

The best service you can provide to your clients and their families is information about resources for driving evaluations and a willingness to provide transportation as one of your services. The fee is a small price to pay for a little peace of mind for all concerned.

A sense of humor is a very helpful and appreciated skill.

This final thought about humor can make life easier for you, your service providers, and your clients. Things just won't always go the way they are supposed to. The client will forget or misunderstand, you will forget or misunderstand, other people will interject themselves into situations and add an unwanted dimension to the moment, and sometimes things just go a little crazy. So, unless the situation is a life threatening one, sometimes just standing back, reflecting with the client and having a good laugh is the best thing that you can do. Sharing a funny story or talking about a fun TV show is also a great way to make life more fun and easier for all. Remember to share a sincere smile as much as possible. It makes a big difference to everyone.

It's not how old you are, it's how you are old."
Jules Renard

www.ingramcontent.com/pod-product-compliance
Lightning Source LLC
Chambersburg PA
CBHW080842170526
45158CB00009B/2609